Clare in the Community

More selfless acts

Clare in the Community

More selfless acts

HARRY VENNING

guardianbooks

First published in 2007 by Guardian Books
119 Farringdon Road, London EC1R 3ER
guardianbooks.co.uk

Guardian Books is an imprint of Guardian News and Media Ltd.

A CIP record for this book is available from the British Library.

ISBN: 978-0-85265-088-2

Cover Design: Two Associates
Text Design: seagulls.net
Printed and bound in Great Britain by Cambridge University Press

To Minnie And Geri, The Super Reds!

1

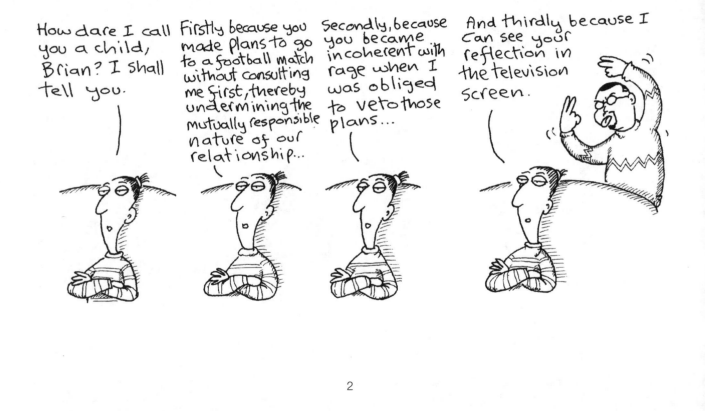

2

The Rose And Crown? Ten minutes? Cheers, Megan. I can't stand another wednesday night in front of the telly, watching Brian get all hot under the collar at the sex scenes in 'ROME'.

See you later, Brian.

That's ridiculous! A woman of her social rank would NEVER make love in the prescence of her servants! WHAT! There is absolutely no historical evidence that Roman women shaved their pubic hair!.... For pity's sake! You wouldn't just throw your toga praetexta on the floor like that, you'd fold it neatly....

5

So, you think the best thing I can do for my kids, to stop them becoming involved in anti-social behaviour and cut down on truency, is to prepare and serve family meals around the dining table.

Absolutely!

OK, I'll try it!

Hey, Kids, has anyone seen the dining table?

11

Hey, Sis, what's up with Abigail?

We had a row. She called me a 'helicopter parent', forever hovering above her, relentlessly pushing her to achieve.

And what did you say to that?

I encouraged her to put her feelings down in writing, maybe work it up into a couple of sample chapters and we can try and get her a book deal.

14

15

What's that music?

Beethoven. The shopping centre plays classical music in the belief it'll disperse groups of youths.

Come on. Let's go. I'm not going to listen to this crap!

Well it seems to work.

Depressing, isn't it. Much as I'd like to think otherwise, I'm afraid kids today are totally predictable, unimaginative and narrow minded.

It's bad enough hearing Beethoven mangled over a tannoy, but this 'Eroica' is the totally lacklustre 1976 Deutsche Grammaphon recording.

Yeah.

22

25

26

This chap is incredible. He has to be the most uncanny 'Stars In Their Eyes' contestant ever!

Close your eyes and you could almost believe you were at an actual Bob Dylan concert.

Doesn't sound anything like him.

The tune is completely unrecognisable.

Fantastic.   Brilliant.

27

So, Brian, was Roy Keane right? Are modern football fans more interested in their prawn sandwich at half-time than in the match?

Of course not! Listen to the roar of the crowd, feel the passion...

...no prawn sandwich can compete with that! Not even a Jamie Oliver one!

Jamie Oliver does a prawn sandwich?

OK, one last time, but pay attention. Fry the garlic and the chillies, add one glass of white wine, then saute the prawns....

Excuse me. I wonder if you could spare a few coins for our Christmas appeal?

Of course. What's Christmas all about, if not remembering those less fortunate than ourselves.

Give the lady a couple of quid, would you Brian.

33

That was a terrible interview. But as a professional I must take full responsibility, identify my mistakes and implement whatever changes are necessary in my attitude and technique.

The one thing I must not do is blame the clients. I mean, its not as if they come here just to make my life a misery.

Well, that was fun. What do you say we all go and piss off the benefits man at the DWP, have some lunch, then drive our housing officer up the wall?

37

39

Excuse the interruption, guys, but I just wanted to stick my head round the door and say "well done" for getting into the spirit of Red Nose Day.

Was that the Alcohol Dependency Group?

Afraid so.

Damn! Damn! Damn! Damn!

Well, I think Harry Potter is brilliant! Not only is Abi still a fan at sixteen, but when a new one comes out she disappears into her room and we don't hear a squeek for hours.

And apparently its just the same with all her friends.

This has long been an area of acute embarrassment here at Mens' group, prompting profound and widespread feelings of shame, emasculation and inadequacy. Well I think it's high time we grabbed the nettle and addressed the issue!

So pay attention, here goes! FIFA Rule 11. A player is in an offside position if: He is nearer to his opponents' goal line than both the ball and the second last opponent. A player is not in an offside position if....

47

48

50

First came CCTV cameras. Then talking CCTV cameras that challenged anti-social behaviour as it was being committed. It was only a matter of time before such powers were abused...

My God! Stripey top with a floral skirt! What were you thinking!!!?

The storyline did present a positive image of the elderly, but in retrospect it was probably a mistake taking the residents to see the latest 'Rocky'.

Poverty, homelessness, debt, organised crime, child labour, prostitution, mental and physical torture, alcoholism ..... the lot!

Thank you, Megan. So, apart from the 'Charles Dickens Theme Park' in Kent, are there any other ideas for this year's Team Day Out?

Whilst it's highly commendable that you want to better understand the contemporary childhood experience, Megan, I think you should give Wayne here his 'heelies' back.

57

OK, at this point I think I should mention a few things. First, I'm not a parent. Second, I've never conducted an ante-natal class and am just covering for a friend...

... and third, I think I may be holding this 'birthing position flash card' upside down.

62

I mean, kids are a lot more sophisticated these days, with a higher tolerance of disturbing imagery. But one really has to question whether this new series of Dr. Who is suitable for an early evening audience.

Just tell me when it's over, Megan.

Oh, my God! They've got into the tardis!!!

Exterminate!

68

Thank heavens for some decent weather. I swear, I'd have gone totally stir-crazy if I'd spent another lunch break cooped up indoors, everyone on top of each other.

Don't get me wrong, Megan, I think it a commendable gesture, and it's to your credit that you want to show solidarity with the disaffected and demonised urban youth...

... I just wonder if this is the best day to wear your hoodie.

Wow, that's a very depressing sight. What do you think caused it?

Poverty.

Poor householders, desperate to save money, employ people on low incomes to do specialist work they're unqualified for. You mark my words, this'll be down to the electrics.

How can you be so sure?

I put them in.

Well, these have been three of the nicest hours I've spent in a long time. There's nothing like a leisurely catch up with an old friend that you have bumped into down at the shops.

The irony is that I only came out to buy one thing, and I can't even remember what it was!!

74

Honestly, Clare, it's brilliant being a social work manager. Getting your way all the time, playing personality politics with the staff, pulling rank, cherry picking the best holiday dates, holding the threat of a bad reference like a weapon...

Helping those in need?

Well, yes, there is that. But every job has its down side.

Well, Brian, I must say I'm pleasantly surprised. To be honest, when I insisted we stop troughing out in front of the telly, and share meals around the dining table instead, I expected you to kick up more of a fuss.....

...especially with The World Cup on.

82

83

84

86

With regional dialects and linguistic idiosyncracies in decline, isn't it rather reassuring to hear some authentic Cockney Rhyming Slang in everyday use!

But what exactly is a Berkeley, and why is he calling you one?

90

91

I'm sorry if you feel I am behaving unfairly and unkindly towards you, Brian, but I did warn you when we first met. Subsequently, I reserve the right to be grumpy and bad tempered in the morning.

But it isn't morning.

It is somewhere.

MANCHESTER UNITED THREE....

Stuff summer! This is what life is all about! Saturday, 4·45pm, Final Score, watching your beloved team's result come in. God is in His heaven, and all's well with the world.

TOTTENHAM HOTSPUR NIL.

You bunch of over paid ****! Call yourselves a ******* football team! You're ****!

Oh no, it's him! Three years ago, when I was in an emotionally vulnerable state, I had a one night stand at this very conference. And he's coming this way!!! How humiliating! This is the worst thing in the world!!!
Oh no, he didn't remember me. He's forgotten our one night stand from only three years ago! How humiliating. This is the worst thing in the world!

95

OK, mytimekeeping does need to improve. And yes, my desk is a mess. Maybe my telephone manner with clients could be less abrupt, and I should work harder to make my case notes a bit more comprehensible.
And you're absolutely right. Unless supervision is totally honest, frank and candid it has no worth. However, in my defence, I would just like to say one thing...
You're the student. I'm supposed to be giving supervision to you.
Oh, I see. Is that how it works?

98

99

Your cultural ignorance astounds me, Clare! I say 'It's the centenary of Laurence Olivier's birth', and you say 'Laurence who?'

Because I never heard of him.

He was the only true genius acting has produced!

The greatest actor of his age, possibly of any age!

Means nothing to me!

He single handedly redefined the actors craft. His sensitivity was beyond compare, his charisma awesome to behold. A colossus! Flawless, peerless, fearless...

Sorry....

He was the really hammy old guy with the ludicrous accent in Marathon Man.

Oh, him.

...and so, yes, I did enter into it with more than a little trepidation but it's amazing how soon you adapt; your cell becomes your home, the 5am starts are actually quite invigorating, the rudimentary diet of beans and rice energises you, and the thrice daily meditation sessions clears your mind of so much clutter its unbelievable, so, on reflection, I'd say that going on a retreat was very worthwhile, although, if I'm honest, I did find it difficult not being allowed to talk for a week...

Harry Venning was born in Wembley in 1959. He has been many things, including an actor, reviewer, illustrator and cartoonist, but he has never been a social worker. He does, however, have his sources in the profession. *Clare in the Community* first appeared in the *Guardian* in 1996, and in 2004 was adapted by Venning and David Ramsden into a Sony award-winning radio sitcom. Three more series have followed.

Harry Venning lives in Brighton, not far from Steve Bell but in a much smaller house.